KOUZES
POSNER

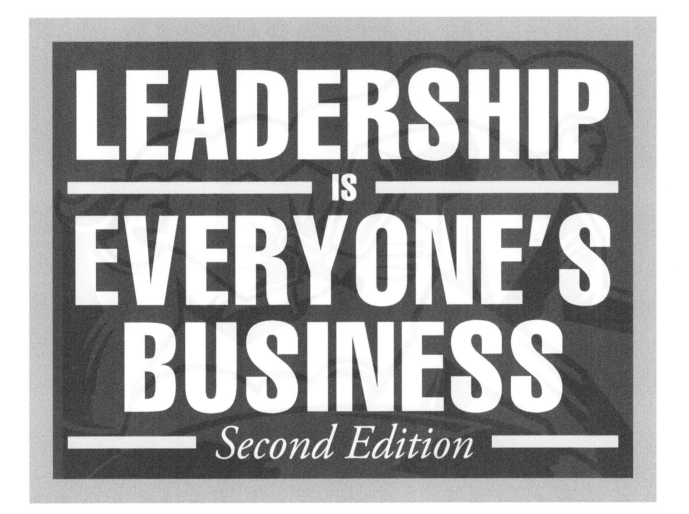

LEADERSHIP
IS
EVERYONE'S
BUSINESS
Second Edition

PARTICIPANT'S WORKBOOK

James M. Kouzes and Barry Z. Posner

CONTENTS

PREFACE

Leadership Is Everyone's Business

More than ever there is a need for people to seize the opportunities that lead us to greatness. Yet, people increasingly ask us, "Why aren't there more leaders?" Why are people reluctant to answer the cry for leadership?

We believe this cautiousness results not from a shortage of courage or competence, but from outdated notions about leadership. In fact, just about every popular notion about leadership is a myth.

While many myths prevail, the most prevalent of all is the idea that leadership is reserved for only a very few of us. This falsehood is perpetuated daily whenever anyone asks, "Are leaders born or made?"

Our research has shown that there is no leadership gene, nor is leadership mystical and ethereal. Leadership is an observable, learnable set of practices. In more than twenty years of research, we've been fortunate to hear and read the stories of thousands of ordinary men and women who have led others to get extraordinary things done. The stories we've collected are not from the famous politicians or corporate CEOs who so often get the credit. They're not from media celebrities or legendary entrepreneurs.

The people we've studied are your neighbors, your colleagues, and your friends. People just like you. These choices are intentional. We want to honor ordinary folks who keep getting extraordinary things done in organizations. Without them—and you—nothing great would ever get done. And if there is one singular lesson about leadership from all of the cases we have gathered, it is this: *leadership is everyone's business.*

Wanting to lead and believing that you can lead are the departure points on the path to leadership development. Stepping out there and exploring the territory, however, is the only way to learn, and that's what *Leadership Is Everyone's Business* is all about. It's a voyage of self-discovery that begins with an expedition into your inner terrain and ends with your commitment to act on what you've learned.

Welcome aboard, and have fun!

Jim Kouzes and Barry Posner

ORIENTEERING

"Our strength as humans and as leaders has nothing to do with what we look like. Rather, it has everything to do with what we feel, what we think of ourselves. . . . Leadership is applicable to all facets of life."

—VERONICA GUERRERO, WINNING EDGE RESEARCH

Places We Have Never Been

"Leadership opportunities are presented to everyone. . . . What makes the difference between being a leader and not is how you respond in the moment.'"

—MICHELE GOINS, CHIEF INFORMATION OFFICER FOR HEWLETT-PACKARD'S IMAGING AND PRINTING GROUP

To *lead*: to go, to guide, to travel

We are all on our way somewhere else. We are all making the journey into a changed world called "the future."

We never travel alone. We have to work together to make our dreams become realities. To make this journey successfully we will all have to become leaders.

This section is called Orienteering, after the sport that's been called "the thinking person's cross-country race." In Orienteering, participants use a compass and a map to set the best and fastest course through unfamiliar territory.

Leadership is a lot like Orienteering. You're expected to find your way through the unknown, and you're expected to help others find theirs. You're expected to participate. There are no spectators in orienteering, and there are no spectators in leadership. Everyone has an important role to play in charting the course to success.

Roving Leadership

Max De Pree, retired chairman and CEO of Herman Miller Inc. and author of *Leadership Is an Art*, talks about "roving leadership." Roving leaders, he says, "are those indispensable people in our lives who take charge when we need them." A roving leader can be anyone who chooses to rise to the occasion based on competence and willingness to take ownership of a problem.

While some leaders hold a position, roving leaders come forward when the situation calls for it.

Here's an example of roving leadership. A customer has a heart attack while waiting in line at the bank. Who's in charge? The bank manager? In all likelihood, a roving leader—a doctor, a nurse, or a bystander trained in CPR—will step forward. Another will call the ambulance. A third will move the crowd back. The situation doesn't call for people with position or authority, but for people with knowledge and initiative.

We're all roving leaders.

In which situation have you or someone you know come forward to assume leadership because the situation called for it?

Workshop Objectives

As a result of participating in the Leadership Is Everyone's Business® Workshop, you will be able to:

- Understand and describe The Five Practices of Exemplary Leadership®.

- Name the essential qualities that people look for and admire in leaders and state the implications for your leadership.

- Understand the meaning and value of individual leadership.

- Identify your own existing leadership strengths and areas for improvement based on your *Leadership Practices Inventory Self-Assessment.*

- Employ at least one method for improving your capacity to engage in each of The Five Practices.

- Create an action plan for taking the next steps in your development as a leader.

My Objectives:

Experience Is the Best Teacher

In our research, we asked people how they learned to lead. According to our study and the findings of other researchers, there are three primary sources of learning:

- Trial and error

- Other people

- Course work and self-study

How We Learn to Lead

Your Personal-Best Leadership Experience is your best lesson in leadership development. Experience—not course work—is the best teacher.

Personal-Best Leadership Experience

In preparing for this workshop, you wrote about your Personal Best as a leader. Take a few moments now to review your notes and get ready to tell your story. Be prepared to hear about some extraordinary accomplishments from your colleagues.

1. **Share your Personal Best.** Take turns telling your stories. When it's your turn, summarize the story to capture the essence of the situation, the key actions, and the leadership lessons.

   As you listen to your colleagues, take notes on the next page about what behaviors, attitudes, and factors seem to be the keys to the success of each leadership event.

   Make sure that someone in each group keeps track of time so that everyone gets a chance to share his or her story completely.

2. **Discuss the stories.** When you've all told your stories, discuss the notes you've made. Share your observations, asking yourself:

   - What do the keys to "Personal-Best Leadership" seem to be?

   - What common elements run through the stories?

   Use page 10 of this workbook to summarize the leadership actions and practices that were common to your group's Personal-Best stories.

3. **Make a flip-chart summary.** List the three to five key common elements in your group's stories that contribute to Personal-Best Leadership. Post the page where all the workshop participants can see it.

Personal-Best Stories: My Observations

When you listen to your colleagues' stories, what behaviors, actions, and attitudes seem to be the keys to their leadership success?

....

....

....

....

....

....

....

....

....

....

Summary of Common Leadership Practices

What common leadership practices, actions, behaviors, or themes run through all the stories?

Leading Your Life

"Leadership is the art of mobilizing others to want to struggle for shared aspirations."

—JIM KOUZES AND BARRY POSNER

In today's fast-moving, complex world, leadership must be everyone's business. At work and home, church and school, we face new and difficult choices. We can't always wait until "the boss" is available to make decisions and take action. We have to be leaders ourselves.

As the saying goes, we "lead" our lives. We call on leadership skills, vision, and teamwork to balance our obligations, ambitions, and resources at work and in the wider world.

Throughout our lives, as we grow and learn and cope with the challenge of change, we don't do it alone. And as we call on others, we use the essential skills of leadership to pursue our goals.

How do you get other people to follow willingly, especially when you set out across unknown territory? How do you mobilize other people to move forward together in a common purpose? How do you persuade others to want to get extraordinary things done?

We interviewed more than five hundred individuals, reviewed more than twelve thousand case studies, and analyzed more than one million survey questionnaires to find out what leaders do to make themselves leaders when performing at their best.

By studying times when leaders performed at their personal best, we were able to identify Five Practices common to most extraordinary leadership achievements.

When leaders are at their best, they:

1. Model the Way
2. Inspire a Shared Vision
3. Challenge the Process
4. Enable Others to Act
5. Encourage the Heart.

The Five Practices of Exemplary Leadership®

- Clarify values by finding your voice and affirming shared ideals.

- Set the example by aligning actions with shared values.

....

....

....

....

- Envision the future by imagining exciting and ennobling possibilities.

- Enlist others in a common vision by appealing to shared aspirations.

....

....

....

....

- Search for opportunities by seizing the initiative and by looking outword for innovative ways to improve.

- Experiment and take risks by constantly generating small wins and learning from experience.

- Foster collaboration by building trust and facilitating relationships.

- Strengthen others by increasing self-determination and developing competence.

- Recognize contributions by showing appreciation for individual excellence.

- Celebrate values and victories by creating a spirit of community.

The Leadership Practices Inventory

What does the LPI measure?

The LPI was developed to validate Jim Kouzes' and Barry Posner's findings from their Personal-Best Leadership case studies. Their goal was to assess the extent to which the behaviors would predict current and future leadership effectiveness. The research data from literally hundreds of thousands of people consistently shows that leaders who engage in the behaviors measured by the LPI are more effective and successful than those who engage in them less frequently.

When you completed the LPI, you used a ten-point scale ranging from "almost never" (1) to "almost always" (10) to indicate how frequently you engage in thirty leadership behaviors, six behaviors for each of The Five Practices. The ranking on one practice does not affect the ranking on any of the others.

The LPI provides information about your perceptions of your leadership behaviors; it does not evaluate your IQ, leadership style, management skill, or personality.

The research demonstrates that increasing the frequency with which you engage in the behaviors measured by the LPI—in other words, The Five Practices—will make you a more effective leader. That's a key objective for this workshop: Learning what The Five Practices of Exemplary Leadership® entail and developing your ability to comfortably engage in them more frequently than you are doing today.

For more about the research, visit www.leadershipchallenge.com.

Scoring Your LPI

1. Take out your LPI and transfer your score for each item to the corresponding item below. Add up the total for each Practice.

2. Graph your score for each Practice on page 17. In the vertical section for each practice, put a dot where your score falls. Then connect the dots.

3. Answer the questions on pages 18 through 20.

Question Number	Model the Way Scores	Notes
1		
6		
11		
16		
21		
26		
TOTAL		

Question Number	Inspire a Shared Vision Scores	Notes
2		
7		
12		
17		
22		
27		
TOTAL		

Question Number	Challenge the Process Scores	Notes
3		
8		
13		
18		
23		
28		
TOTAL		

Question Number	Enable Others to Act Scores	Notes
4		
9		
14		
19		
24		
29		
TOTAL		

Question Numbers	Encourage the Heart Scores	Notes
5		
10		
15		
20		
25		
30		
TOTAL		

Graphing Your LPI Scores

Leadership Practices Inventory (LPI) Percentile Ranking

Percentile	Model the Way	Inspire a Shared Vision	Challenge the Process	Enable Others to Act	Encourage the Heart
100	60	60	60	60	60
.			59		
.	59	59			
.			58		
.	58	58	57	59	59
.		57			
.					58
90	57	56	56	58	
.			55		57
.	56	55			
.				57	
.	55	54	54		56
80			53	56	55
.	54	53			
.					54
.			52		
.	53	52		55	
70			51		53
.		51			
.	52			54	
.		50	50		52
.	51				
.		49			51
60	50		49	53	
.					50
.		48	48	52	
.	49	47			49
.			47		
50		46		51	48
.	48		46		
.		45			
.					47
.	47	44	45	50	
.					46
40	46	43	44	49	45
.	45	42	43		
.		41		48	44
.	44		42		43
30	43	40	41	47	42
.		39	40	46	41
.	42	38			40
.	41	37	39	45	39
.		36	38	44	38
20	40	35	37	43	37
.	39	34	36		
.	38	33		42	36
.	37	32	35 34	41	35
.	36	31 30	33	40	34 33
10	35	29	32	39 38	32
.	34	28	31		31
.	33	27	30	37	29 30
.	32	25 26	29	35 36	28
.	31	24	27 28	34	27
.	29 30	22 23	26	32 33	25 26
.	28	21	24 25	30 31	23 24
.	25 - 27	18 - 20	22 23	28 29	20 - 22
.	22 - 24	16 17	18 -21	24 - 27	17 - 19
1	19 - 21	13 - 15	16 17	19 - 23	11 - 16

Making Sense of Your LPI Scores

Strengths

On which Practice did you score highest? This is the one with which you feel the most comfortable.

What do you think are your strengths as a leader? Which leadership behaviors are most comfortable for you to use? Why? How do you use them in your job?

Statement # _____.

....

Statement # _____.

....

Statement # _____.

....

Statement # _____.

....

Statement # _____.

....

Opportunities

On which Practice did you score the lowest? This is the one with which you feel the least comfortable.

With your new and increased awareness about leadership, what are five specific leadership behaviors that you would like to engage in more frequently? Why?

Statement # _____.

....

Statement # _____.

....

Statement # _____.

....

Statement # _____.

....

Statement # _____.

....

Action Steps

- What actions would you like to take in the near future to improve your leadership ability?

- How might you apply the leadership practices in your job? Be as specific as possible.

Orienteering Summary

At the beginning of any journey, it's critical to get your bearings. That's what we've done in this module. We've oriented ourselves to the landscape of leadership. We've also discovered that each of us has a Personal-Best Leadership Experience that provides a foundation for our development, taken a close look at our strengths and opportunities to improve, and identified some actions we can take to improve our leadership abilities.

Key Learnings

- Leadership is everyone's business.

- Leadership development is self-development.

- Leadership is a set of skills and abilities that can be learned.

- Leadership development is not an event; it's an ongoing process.

Time to Reflect

If you were to leave the workshop now, what is the most significant lesson you learned about yourself as a leader?

....

....

....

....

"How many leaders will one organization need? A lot must be the answer, lots of them all over the place."

**—CHARLES HANDY,
AUTHOR OF *THE AGE OF UNREASON***

PRACTICE 1
MODEL THE WAY

"If you want to lead others . . . you have to open up your heart . . . you have to be able to be honest with yourself in order to be honest with others."

—NEVZAT MERT TOPCU,
FOUNDER OF *AW MAGAZINE* ABOUT PC GAMES IN TURKEY

Model the Way

To model effectively, you must first believe in something. A leader needs a personal philosophy that serves to guide decisions and actions, a set of values about how people ought to be treated.

Leaders must be clear about their guiding principles and then speak clearly and distinctly about what they believe. They also forge agreement about a set of common principles and ideas that make the organization unique and distinctive.

But eloquent words about your personal values are not enough. Leaders stand up for their beliefs. They practice what they preach. They show others by their own example that they live on a daily basis. Leaders know it is their behavior that earns them respect. It is the consistency of word and deed that builds credibility.

Model the Way
Commitments

- Clarify values by finding your voice and affirming shared values.

- Set the example by aligning actions with shared values.

Characteristics of Admired Leaders

Percentage of Respondents Who Selected the Characteristic as One of the Seven Qualities They Most Admire in a Leader

This Group	Norms		This Group	Norms	
_____	28	**Ambitious** (aspiring, hardworking, striving)	_____	84	**Honest** (truthful, has integrity, trustworthy, has character)
_____	40	**Broad-minded** (open-minded, flexible, receptive, tolerant)	_____	17	**Imaginative** (creative, innovative, curious)
_____	23	**Caring** (appreciative, compassionate, concerned, loving, nurturing)	_____	5	**Independent** (self-reliant, self-sufficient, self-confident)
_____	66	**Competent** (capable, proficient, effective, efficient, professional)	_____	66	**Inspiring** (uplifting, enthusiastic, energetic, humorous, cheerful, positive about the future)
_____	31	**Cooperative** (collaborative, team player, responsive)	_____	47	**Intelligent** (bright, thoughtful, intellectual, reflective, logical)
_____	22	**Courageous** (bold, daring, fearless, gutsy)	_____	18	**Loyal** (faithful, dutiful, unswerving in allegiance, devoted)
_____	39	**Dependable** (reliable, conscientious, responsible)	_____	17	**Mature** (experienced, wise, has depth)
_____	22	**Determined** (dedicated, resolute, persistent, purposeful)	_____	10	**Self-controlled** (restrained, self-disciplined)
_____	35	**Fair-minded** (just, unprejudiced, objective, forgiving, willing to pardon others)	_____	32	**Straightforward** (direct, candid, forthright)
_____	62	**Forward-looking** (visionary, foresighted, concerned about the future, sense of direction)	_____	37	**Supportive** (helpful, offers assistance, comforting)

What Constituents Expect of Leaders

Managers are appointed. Leaders, however, are chosen by their constituents. Leadership is earned, not given.

Most of us look for some special qualities in leaders. Over the past twenty years, the Characteristics of an Admired Leader questionnaire described on the previous page has been completed by hundreds of thousands people worldwide. Respondents are asked to select seven of the twenty given characteristics that best define leadership that they would choose to follow. Consistently, people select the same four characteristics:

Characteristics of Admired Leaders

....

....

Taken together, the four characteristics that constituents expect of leaders add up to what communications experts refer to as **source credibility**. According to communications experts, a source of information is considered believable when he or she is considered to possess the following three characteristics.

Components of Source Credibility

....

....

Credibility

Credibility has a deep impact on organizations. When we studied the credibility of hundreds of leaders in dozens of organizations, we found that people who perceive their leaders to have high credibility are more likely to:

- Be proud to say they're part of the organization.

- Feel a strong sense of team spirit.

- See their own personal values as consistent with those of the organization.

- Feel attached and committed to the organization.

- Have a sense of ownership of the organization.

Their studies also found that when constituents perceive their leaders to have low credibility, they're significantly more likely to:

- Produce only if they're watched carefully.

- Are motivated primarily by money.

- Say good things about the organization publicly, but criticize it privately.

- Consider looking for another job in tough times.

- Feel unsupported and unappreciated.

How do leaders earn this valuable credibility? What is credibility behaviorally?

_____ _____ _____ _____ _____ _____ _____

Clarify Your Values

Values help us determine what to do and what not to do. They're the deep-seated, pervasive standards that influence every aspect of our lives: our moral judgments, our responses to others, and our commitments to personal and organizational goals. Values set parameters for the hundreds of decisions we make every day. Options that run counter to our value system are seldom acted upon; if they are, it's done with a sense of compliance rather than commitment. Values constitute our personal bottom line.

What's the impact of values clarity on commitment? Let's take a look:

"We lead from the essence of who we are."

**—LILLAS BROWN,
UNIVERSITY OF SASKATCHEWAN**

Defining Your Values

Clarification of values begins with becoming more self-aware. What values are important to you? What are the strongly held principles you believe should guide your daily decisions and actions at work?

____ Achievement/Success	____ Flexibility	____ Power
____ Autonomy	____ Friendship	____ Productivity
____ Beauty	____ Freedom	____ Prosperity/Wealth
____ Challenge	____ Growth	____ Quality
____ Communication	____ Happiness	____ Recognition
____ Competence	____ Harmony	____ Respect
____ Competition	____ Health	____ Risk Taking
____ Courage	____ Honesty/Integrity	____ Security
____ Creativity	____ Hope	____ Service
____ Curiosity	____ Humor	____ Simplicity
____ Decisiveness	____ Independence	____ Spirituality/Faith
____ Dependability	____ Innovation	____ Strength
____ Discipline	____ Intelligence	____ Teamwork
____ Diversity	____ Love/Affection	____ Trust
____ Effectiveness	____ Loyalty	____ Truth
____ Empathy	____ Open-Mindedness	____ Variety
____ Equality	____ Patience	____ Wisdom
____ Family		

Shared Values Make a Difference

When team members share a common set of values, the payoff is awesome. In studying more than three thousand managers around the country in partnership with Warren Schmidt, we found that people feel differently about the organization when clear, strong values are shared across the board. Shared values make a significant difference in work attitudes and performance.

Shared Values Make a Difference Because They:

- Foster strong feelings of personal effectiveness.

- Promote high levels of company loyalty.

- Facilitate consensus about key organizational goals and stakeholders.

- Encourage ethical behavior.

- Promote strong norms about working hard and caring.

- Reduce levels of job stress and tension.

- Foster pride in the organization.

- Facilitate understanding about job expectations.

- Foster teamwork and esprit de corps.

In good times, shared values are a common language for expressing standards and ambitions. They can be the beacon that lights the way in less clear, more troubled times.

> "Shared values are the glue that holds this organization together."
>
> **—SHELLY BROWN,**
> **ASPECT TELECOMMUNICATIONS**

Shared Values Notes

How a Leader Models the Way

Think of a leader you know or have known.

- What one or two core values does or did that leader espouse?

- What did you see that leader do to demonstrate commitment to his or her values?

- How closely does (or did) the actions taken by that leader align with those core values?

- How do (or did) people respond to this leader?

Values/Standards What Is Professed as Being Important (Say)	Actions What Is Actually Practiced (Do)

Model the Way Summary

- Clarify values by finding your voice and affirming shared values.

- Set the example by aligning actions with shared values.

Key Learnings

Leadership development is a journey of life-long learning that begins with a focus on yourself. In order to lead, you must . . .

- Be credible or believable in order to enlist the support of others.

- Be clear on your own key values, beliefs, and principles and let others know what they are.

- Lead by example—take stands on important issues and act consistently with your stated values and intentions.

Time to Reflect

- Where are you on your journey to become a better leader?

- What are the two most important things you learned about the practice of Model the Way?

- How clear are you on your values and the guiding principles that govern your decisions and actions?

....

....

"I never asked anyone to do anything I wouldn't or couldn't do myself."

— MARY GODWIN, RADIUS

PRACTICE 2
INSPIRE A SHARED VISION

"Never mistake a clear view for a short distance."

—PAUL SAFFO, TECHNOLOGY FORECASTER AND PROFESSOR, STANFORD UNIVERSITY

Inspire a Shared Vision

There is no freeway to the future, no paved highway from here to tomorrow. There is only wilderness, uncertain terrain. There are no road maps, no signposts. Like explorers, leaders have their skills and experience to prepare them. And while explorers rely on their compasses to determine direction, leaders steer by their dreams.

Leaders look forward to the future. They gaze across the horizon of time, imagining the opportunities that are in store once they and their constituents arrive at their destination. They have a sense of purpose. They are unceasingly positive about the future, and they passionately believe that people can make a difference.

Leaders share their dreams. They breathe life into their visions and communicate these visions so that others understand and accept them. They forge unity of purpose by showing constituents how the dream is for the common good. They communicate their passion through vivid language and expressive style.

Inspire a Shared Vision Commitments

- Envision the future by imagining exciting and ennobling possibilities.

- Enlist others in a common vision by appealing to shared aspirations.

"I Have a Dream"

As you listen to Martin Luther King, Jr.'s speech, make notes on what makes it an inspiring presentation. Pay attention to what Dr. King says and to the communication methods and styles he uses. (For a link to audio of Dr. Martin Luther King, Jr.'s "I Have a Dream" speech, we suggest searching YouTube® or your preferred online source for audio files.)

What Is a Vision?

A vision pulls people forward. It projects a clear image of a possible future. It generates the enthusiasm and energy to strive toward the goal.

> A vision is an IDEAL and UNIQUE IMAGE of the FUTURE for the COMMON GOOD.

All inspiring visions include these components:

- IDEAL (a high standard to aspire to). Visions are about hopes, dreams, and aspirations. They're about exciting possibilities. They're about making a difference, creating something grand, achieving a whole new standard of excellence. They tell us the ennobling purpose and greater good we are seeking.

....

....

....

....

- UNIQUE (pride in being different, an identity). Visions are about the extraordinary, not the ordinary. They're not about how we are like everyone else, but about how we are different and special. They are about what makes us distinctive, singular, and unequaled.

....

....

....

....

- **IMAGE** (a concept or mental picture made real or tangible through descriptive language). We remember our past and project our future in mental pictures. Word pictures, metaphors, analogies, examples, stories, symbols, and similar communication methods all help make visions memorable.

....

....

....

- **FUTURE-ORIENTED** (looking toward a destination). A vision is a description of an exciting possibility that we desire in the future. If it were a description of what exists today, it wouldn't be a vision; it'd be reality. Visions are projections. They stretch our minds out into the future and ask us to dream. The horizons of visions vary, but generally speaking, five to ten years is a reasonable time horizon.

....

....

....

- **COMMON GOOD** (a way people can come together). Visions are about developing a shared sense of destiny. They are about what the group or organization or community members collectively desire. Visions aren't about what the leader wants. They are about what we want. Leaders must be able to show others how their interests are served and how they are a part of the vision in order to enlist others in it.

....

....

....

Giving the Vision Life

A vision can't really be conveyed by memo. It is best communicated in person. The message has more meaning when conveyed by someone whose enthusiasm shows in a smile, in gestures. Audiences respond better when you speak clearly and quickly and make eye contact. These details convey your excitement and conviction, which are likely to spread to the audience.

Read these two visions and ask yourself which would inspire you to sign on.

_____ Vision 1: "At Widget International it is our stated goal to be competitive within the industry on price and quality."

_____ Vision 2: "In our hearts, minds, guts, and muscle . . . we stand for bringing computer power to the people so they can share in the fun."

The statement in Vision 2 was made by Jean-Louis Gassee, senior vice president of research and development at Apple Computer. This example is really just the start, as it captures the essence of a vision in an interesting and compelling way. Leaders learn how to elaborate on their vision, much in the same way Dr. Martin Luther King, Jr., spoke of freedom in many variations during his speech. Let's turn to the next page to start.

Give the Vision Life

The literal definition of the word inspire is "to breathe life into." To enlist others in a common purpose, leaders breathe life into the vision and animate it so that others can see it, hear it, taste it, touch it, and feel it. In making the intangible vision tangible, leaders engage their constituents and ignite commitment.

By using powerful images, positive communication styles, and verbal expressiveness, leaders bring their visions alive for others.

Breathe life into your vision by using:

- Metaphors and analogies

- Examples, stories, and humor

- Word pictures

- Slogans, theme songs

- Poetry and quotations

- Pictures and symbols

In order to enlist the support of others in your vision, convey your confidence and energy in the kind of language you use:

- Assured

- Optimistic

- Active

- Realistic

Envisioning Our Team's Future

Work with your colleagues to do some creative thinking about your shared vision of an ideal future for your team or group. Your goal is to draw a picture that represents an **ideal future** for your team or develop an "ad" that presents your team as you would like to be seen by co-workers and customers. Then communicate your vision to the others in the workshop.

Instructions

1. Take two to three minutes of quiet time to reflect on how your group can contribute to your organization's vision and goals. What are your strengths? Opportunities? What are you enthusiastic about? What visual ideas might capture your idea of "who we want to be"?

....

....

....

....

....

2. In small groups discuss with your team which of the options below, **A** or **B**, to choose and which team objective or goal to focus on.

   Option A: Draw a picture of an **ideal future** for your team as you work to achieve your organization's values, mission, or objectives. How will your team demonstrate leadership in this area? What image could reflect your new role and way of working together?

   Option B: Develop a **"corporate ad"** that presents your team as you would like to be seen by co-workers and customers in the future. Tie your image to the organization's mission or objectives. Your ad should include a visual element as well as a "headline" or slogan. Focus on an image or picture that captures your ideal new role and way of working together.

3. Brainstorm symbols or visual images that capture your team's role and spirit. Be creative and encourage everyone to contribute.

4. Once you've chosen the team objective or goal you would like to focus on and Option A or B for presenting your vision, begin planning. Divide the project into smaller tasks so that each person has a role. Take several minutes and sketch some images. A tree? A map? A bird? A socket wrench? A pair of binoculars? Lay out your design on the flip chart at your table.

5. Working together, make the most dynamic and appealing picture or ad you can. Use the remainder of your time to plan a presentation to the rest of the group.

6. Present your design to the larger group and explain what it represents.

"Leaders have their heads in the clouds and their feet on the ground. That way they can still envision the summit, but ascend it by putting one foot in front of the other."

—JIM KOUZES AND BARRY POSNER

Envisioning Our Team's Future: Notes and Sketches

Inspire a Shared Vision Summary

- Envision the future by imagining exciting and ennobling possibilities.

- Enlist others in a common vision by appealing to shared aspirations.

Key Learnings

- To help everyone in the organization see clearly what's ahead, leaders must have, and clearly convey, a vision.

- Leaders give everyone a sense of what the future will look like.

- Leaders breathe life into their visions and enlist others by showing how those visions serve their own values and interests.

Time to Reflect

What are the two most important things you learned about the practice Inspire a Shared Vision?

How clear are you about the important themes and the higher-order values that give your life and work meaning and direction?

> "I paint pictures, try to bring the idea to life, over and over again."

**—SIEGFRIED MEISTER,
RATIONAL GROSSKÜCHENTECHNIK GMBH**

PRACTICE 3
CHALLENGE THE PROCESS

"Sometimes you just can't predict where the change will come from, but you have to have your eyes open if you have any hope of even catching a glimpse of it."

—MICHAEL PRIEST,
CEO OF BAY AREA CREDIT SERVICES

Challenge the Process

Challenge is the opportunity for greatness. As you saw in the Personal-Best activity, people do their best when there's the chance to change the way things are. Leaders welcome opportunities to test their abilities. They look for innovative ways to improve their work and their organizations.

Leaders venture out. They don't sit idly waiting for fate to smile on them. They create opportunities for small wins that add up to major victories. They are pioneers—people who are willing to step out into the unknown.

Great leaders are great learners. They know that risk taking involves mistakes and failure, so they accept the inevitable disappointments and treat them as learning opportunities. They are willing to experiment and take risks in order to find new and better ways of doing things. Leaders also create safe environments in which others can learn from their failures as well as their successes.

Challenge
the Process
Commitments

- Search for opportunities by seizing the initiative and by looking outward for innovative ways to improve.

- Experiment and take risks by constantly generating small wins and learning from experience.

Recalling a Challenge

Have you ever jumped out of an airplane? Rappelled down a cliff? Marched in a protest? Stood up to your boss? Gone out on a limb for an important project? Select a memorable occasion when you really stretched yourself to try something new, to take a risk, to Challenge the Process. Then answer the questions below.

1. Briefly describe the action you took.

----

2. What specific risks did you take? What did you stand to lose?

----

3. What did stretching yourself feel like? How would you compare your feelings before, during, and after the experience?

....

....

....

----

4. What did you stand to gain from taking this risk? What motivated you to move through the obstacles?

....

....

....

----

5. What support did you ask for or receive from others that helped you take the risk?

....

....

....

Opportunities for Challenge

Challenge typically arises from three kinds of situations—things that aren't working, are broken, or need fixing; brand new initiatives; and obstacles that keep us from achieving our visions. They can also be the situations that are keeping us from realizing the vision we described in the previous section.

List three opportunities for challenge in your organization. The categories listed below may help stimulate your thinking.

Ineffective policies/procedures	Strategies that are not working
Commonplace bad behaviors	Practices that irritate customers
Projects needing redirection	Reports we don't use
Systems that do not work	Mediocre results that we accept
Work that does not add value	Useless or ineffective meetings

1. _____

2. _____

3. _____

Now list three opportunities to pursue. The following items may help inspire you:

New markets and/or products	New customer groups
New technologies	New behavioral or cultural norms
New competitive strategies	New performance goals
New systems processes	New policies or procedures
New projects	New organizational structure

1. _____

2. _____

3. _____

Stretching Toward Our Visions

Challenging the Process is stretching yourself—and your team—beyond your comfort zone. Achieving a future that is beyond today's reality requires us to stretch: to actively seek out opportunities that move us toward the vision, and to experiment with new ideas and approaches. In this activity, you will use your own experience of challenging to help you identify ways you can "stretch" as a team.

1. Discuss your individual observations about experiencing challenge. Be sure each team member has a chance to speak.

2. Look at the picture you drew or the ad you created earlier to convey your vision and your ideas from "I'm Up for the Challenge." Share your ideas with your team. Be sure all your team members have an opportunity to share their ideas.

3. As a team, select two or three challenges that:

    ■ You are enthusiastic about

    ■ Would result in real progress toward the vision

    ■ You can accomplish alone with a minimum of resources and approvals

4. Select one specific challenge from the list above that you will focus on personally. Tell your teammates:

    ■ What precisely you plan to do

    ■ Why this action will move the team closer to its vision

    ■ Why this action is a challenge for you

Generate Small Wins

Small wins create a pattern of winning that attracts people who want to be allied with a successful venture. Leaders identify the place to start and begin by modeling action. Breaking big, even overwhelming, problems into small, manageable chunks is an important aspect of creating small wins. Leaders work hard at finding ways to make it easy for the team to succeed.

What makes small wins so successful in creating momentum for change? Use the space below to record ideas from your colleagues.

Key Actions for Generating Small Wins

- Break it down. Break big problems down into small, doable pieces.

- Make a model. Create a small-scale version of what you're trying to do so you can see whether it will work.

- Keep it simple. Your visions should be grand, but keep your actions as simple as possible.

- Do the easy parts first. Help the group discover that they can do it.

- Accumulate *yeses*. Ask for agreement to do the first thing, then the second, then the third, and so on.

- Experiment. Try, fail, learn, and then try again.

- Give feedback. Let people know how they are doing.

- Celebrate. When you reach milestones, take the time to congratulate one another.

Challenge the Process Summary

- Search for opportunities by seizing the initiative and by looking outward for innovative ways to improve.

- Experiment and take risks by constantly generating small wins and learning from experience.

Key Learnings

- Leadership is closely associated with change and innovation.

- Leaders actively seek and create new opportunities within the context of their values and vision.

- Leaders experiment and take risks. They see mistakes as opportunities to learn, and they help others generate small wins and learn from their mistakes.

Time to Reflect

- What are the two most important things you learned about the practice of Challenge the Process?

- Where can you look for creative, innovative ideas for addressing your challenges?

....

....

....

PRACTICE 4
ENABLE OTHERS TO ACT

"The best way for me to give power to other people . . . is to allow creativity and freedom to explore new ideas and ways of thinking."

—JILL CLEVELAND,
FINANCE MANAGER OF APPLE, INC.

Enable Others to Act

Leaders don't travel alone. They foster collaboration. They nurture self-esteem in others and make them feel strong and capable. Leaders make sure that when they win, everybody wins.

Leaders make co-workers feel like co-owners, not hired hands. They help to build teams with spirit and cohesion, teams that have a true sense of community. Leaders involve others in making plans and decisions and develop collaborative goals and cooperative relationships.

Leaders strengthen and develop others by sharing power and information and by giving others visibility and credit. As coaches and teachers, they give others challenging tasks and support them with the tools they need to be successful. Leaders clear obstacles from others' paths.

Enable Others to Act Commitments

- Foster collaboration by building trust and facilitating relationships.

- Strengthen others by increasing self-determination and developing competence.

Powerful Times, Powerless Times

Think of a time or times when you felt powerful as a result of what someone said or did. Describe specifically what the person said or did.

....

....

....

....

Think of a time or times when you felt powerless as a result of what someone said or did. Describe specifically what the person said or did.

....

....

....

....

Reflect back on the "powerful" and "powerless" lists from the previous page.

Now think about your actions with others in your workplace. Consider the following questions:

- What things have you said or done recently to *enable* others? Be as specific as you can.

....

....

....

- What things have you said or done recently that might have been *disabling* to others? Be specific.

....

....

....

- What barriers get in the way of enabling others? What can you do to remove or reduce these barriers?

....

....

....

Strengthening Others

Research reveals a vital lesson that everyone should take to heart: the more people believe that they can influence and control their work, the greater organizational effectiveness and individual satisfaction will be. In other words, choice and latitude result in higher job fulfillment and performance.

Here are some ideas for helping to give others more control over their work and helping them feel more capable:

- Share information.

- Listen actively to other points of view.

- Involve others in planning and decision making.

- Give credit for ideas and contributions to the team effort.

- Teach others what you know.

- Help others clear away obstacles.

Add Your Own

Developing Cooperative Goals and Roles

Shared goals and shared roles bind people together in collaborative pursuits. As individuals work together and recognize that they need each other in order to be successful, they become convinced that everyone should contribute and that, by cooperating, they can accomplish the task successfully.

Reflect on a situation in your organization that could benefit from more cooperative behavior. Perhaps it's the design of a new product, a solution to a customer service problem, or a new approach to increasing sales.

- What could you do to foster collaboration?

- How could you help ensure that every member of the team contributes to the success so that no one wins unless everyone wins?

Situation: _____

Ideas for fostering collaboration:

....

....

....

....

....

Enable Others to Act Summary

- Foster collaboration by building trust and facilitating relationships.

- Strengthen others by increasing self-determination and developing competence.

Key Learnings

"You can't do it alone" is a mantra of the most exemplary leaders. You simply can't get extraordinary things done by yourself. Leaders . . .

- Know that collaboration enables teams, partnerships, and other alliances to function effectively.

- Know that teams can't function without strong individuals.

- Make people feel capable of acting on their own initiative.

- Use their power in service of others because they know that capable, confident people perform better.

Time to Reflect

What are the two most important things you learned about the practice of Enable Others to Act?

What's the relationship between the level of the challenge and the level of your competencies and skills within your team?

....

....

PRACTICE 5
ENCOURAGE THE HEART

"A sincere word of thanks from the right person at the right time can mean more to an employee than a raise, a formal award, or a whole wall of certificates and plaques."

—BOB NELSON,
1001 WAYS TO REWARD EMPLOYEES

Encourage the Heart

Getting extraordinary things done in organizations is hard work. The climb to the summit is arduous and long. People become exhausted, frustrated, and disenchanted. They're often tempted to give up. Leaders Encourage the Heart of their constituents to carry on. They inspire others with courage and hope.

To keep hope and determination alive, leaders recognize contributions by showing appreciation for individual excellence. Genuine acts of caring uplift spirits and strengthen courage.

On every winning team, the members need to share in the rewards of their efforts. So leaders celebrate the values and the victories by creating a spirit of community. They express pride in the accomplishments of their team, and they make everyone feel like everyday heroes.

Encourage the Heart Commitments

- Recognize contributions by showing appreciation for individual excellence.

- Celebrate the values and victories by creating a spirit of community.

Most Meaningful Recognition

Think about one of the most meaningful recognitions you have ever received. It can be related to any part of your life—work, family, school, or community.

- What was the recognition?

- Why did you receive it?

- What made it so meaningful to you?

- Focus on behaviors. What did others say or do?

- What are some of the common elements that you heard from your colleagues' most meaningful recognition stories?

- List some of your group's most important elements for creating meaningful recognition.

....

....

....

....

The Four Essentials of Encouraging the Heart

Expect the Best

Successful leaders have high expectations of themselves and of others. People frequently step up to higher levels of performance when expectations are high. Leaders bring out the best in others by making sure that people know what is expected of them and by encouraging them to be their best.

....

....

....

....

Personalize Recognition

Leaders pay attention to remarkable achievements as well as achievements that are relatively small in scope, yet are personal breakthroughs, and recognize them. A cornerstone of meaningful recognition is that it is perceived as personal. For example, leaders tell stories with vivid details that reinforce why a person is being recognized. Many corporate recognition programs are ineffective because everyone receives the same recognition (such as a gift certificate) for very different accomplishments. Personalized recognition lets people know they are valued as unique individuals and that their leaders have a thoughtful and personal interest in their accomplishments.

....

....

....

....

Create a Spirit of Community

Leaders not only recognize individual excellence, but they celebrate team values and victories. Celebrating together creates a heightened sense of community, belonging, and inclusion. It sends a message that everyone benefits when great things occur and reminds people of the enormous potential of what can be accomplished together.

....

....

....

....

Be Personally Involved

You cannot delegate affairs of the heart. As a leader you must search for examples of people doing things right. You must be willing to look people in the eye and thank them. You must be personally involved with people, so that you know when they are worthy of special recognition or need reassurance or guidance when they have tough work to do. Your acts of encouragement send very clear messages about the importance and legitimacy of what people do.

Practicing Recognition

Think of someone who helped you in some way, either recently or in the past, but whom you neglected to thank. Take a few moments to write the thank-you note you should have sent at that time. Seriously consider sending the note to the person after this workshop ends.

How did you show recognition in your note?

....

....

....

....

How does it feel to express your gratitude?

....

....

....

....

Why did you not express it at the time of the incident?

....

....

....

....

What are the benefits of letting others know that their actions or statements were helpful to you?

....

....

....

....

Encourage the Heart Idea Exchange

Earlier in this session you shared your Most Meaningful Recognition. We saw from that experience that there are many creative ways to recognize others and to celebrate achievements. (In fact, many books have been written listing hundreds of ways to do this.)

Use the space below to add a few more ideas that will Encourage the Heart.

Encourage the Heart Summary

- Recognize contributions by showing appreciation for individual excellence.

- Celebrate the values and victories by creating a spirit of community.

Key Learnings

The root of the word "encourage" means heart. Leaders understand that in order to accomplish the extraordinary, people must have strong and committed hearts. When offering encouragement to another person, the leader is, in fact, providing courage and strength to that person's heart.

To keep people inspired and willing to persevere on the long and challenging path to success, leaders:

- Constantly recognize excellence of individuals and teams.

- Provide support and encouragement to express their belief and confidence in others.

- Show their appreciation for big and small things people do to achieve goals and model values.

Time to Reflect

What are the two most important things you learned about the practice of Encourage the Heart?

....

....

....

....

....

- ■ Which of your team members would really benefit from more recognition?

....

....

....

....

....

COMMITTING

"Leadership requires learning on the job. With the will power—and the heart—to continue, you can lead the way."

—CHRISTIAN FUX,
INTERNATIONAL COMMITTEE OF THE RED CROSS, KENYA

Committing

Every exceptional leader is an exceptional learner. The self-confidence required to lead comes from learning about ourselves—our skills, knowledge, prejudices, talents, and shortcomings. Self-confidence develops as we build our strengths and overcome weaknesses.

Many leadership skills can be learned successfully in the classroom, but we also learn from other people and from experiences. We must take advantage of every opportunity to practice our skills. We may fail, but we will learn from our mistakes.

Ultimately, leadership development is self-development. Musicians have their instruments. Engineers have their computers. Accountants have their calculators. Leaders have themselves. They are their own instruments.

In this section you will make firm and specific commitments to act on what you've learned about leadership.

Committing
Objectives

■ Identify your strengths and areas for improvement within each of The Five Practices.

■ Identify one action that you will take for each of The Five Practices to improve your leadership abilities.

My Leadership Assessment

Reflect back on your LPI scores and Personal-Best Leadership Experience, along with your insights from activities and experiences you've engaged in during this workshop. Then use the space below to summarize your strengths and areas for improvement in each of The Five Practices.

1 MODEL the Way

- Clarify values
- Set the example

_____
_____
_____
_____
_____
_____
_____
_____

2 INSPIRE a Shared Vision

- Envision the future
- Enlist others

_____
_____
_____
_____
_____
_____
_____
_____

3 CHALLENGE
the Process

- Search for opportunities
- Experiment and take risks

_____
_____
_____
_____
_____
_____
_____

4 ENABLE
Others to Act

- Foster collaboration
- Strengthen others

_____
_____
_____
_____
_____
_____
_____

5 ENCOURAGE
the Heart

- Recognize contributions
- Celebrate values and victories

_____
_____
_____
_____
_____
_____
_____

My Commitments to Action

Consider The Five Practices and The Ten Commitments of Leadership from the previous pages.

- ■ What one action for each of The Five Practices of will you take within the next thirty days in order to increase the likelihood that others will see you as a leader and choose to join in your efforts?

Refer to "Suggestions for Becoming a Better Leader" and "The Journey Continues" sections in the Appendix of this workbook to help spark some ideas.

Sign and date this page to show you are committed to acting on your plan.

Leadership Practice	One Action I Will Take	Other People to Involve
Model the Way		
Inspire a Shared Vision		
Challenge the Process		
Enable Others to Act		
Encourage the Heart		

Signed:_____

APPENDIX

Suggestions for Becoming a Better Leader

Model the Way

- Set an example for others by behaving in ways that demonstrate and reinforce your stated values.

- Work with people. You can't set an example by working alone.

- Publicize your "rules of the road." Live by them. If top quality is your priority, don't **ever** let a single flaw pass you by without comment and action.

- Talk with others about your values and beliefs. Be expressive (even emotional) about them. If you're proud of your co-workers for living up to high performance standards, let them know. Then go brag about it to others.

- Tell stories about people who are living the values in memorable ways.

Inspire a Shared Vision

- Develop a vision for today. Ask yourself, "Am I in the job to do something or am I in it for something to do?" Make a list of what you want to accomplish while you are in your current job—and why.

- Keep refining and updating your vision. Write an article about how you have made a difference. Date it for three years from today. Be bold and imagine the best of yourself.

- Learn how to communicate your vision effectively. Join Toastmasters. Take a course in effective presentations.

- Make time each week to find out about future trends in your industry and your world. Join the World Futures

Society. Read *American Demographics* or other magazines about future trends. Use the Internet to find a "futures" conference that you can attend. Make a list of what reputable people are predicting will happen in the next ten years.

■ Set time aside every week to talk about the future with co-workers. Make your vision of the future part of the staff meeting, a working lunch, and conversations by the water cooler, etc.

■ Listen—and learn. Ask your colleagues about their dreams, plans, and goals. Talk them over. Incorporate them into your group's vision.

Challenge the Process

■ Choose one routine task, and do it as if it were the first time. Ask yourself fundamental questions. Why am I doing this? Why does it have to be done this way?

■ Ask for a tough assignment.

■ Find something that's broken and fix it. Is it your calculator or is it your compensation system?

■ Set up a small experiment. Do something in a new and more effective way.

■ Collect new ideas. Start an idea club. Ask everyone on the team to come in with one new idea to improve the team's work.

■ Enroll in a class, course, or workshop dealing with a subject that you don't know anything about.

■ Ask why. Next time you don't understand a policy or procedure, make sure you get an explanation—or a change!

■ Stand up for your beliefs, even if you're a minority of one.

Enable Others to Act

- Always say "we." It's only a token of commitment to teamwork and sharing, but it will be noticed and valued.

- Create interactions. By bringing people together, you develop teamwork and trust. Bring a colleague along to the next meeting at headquarters. Attend a meeting or workshop with a colleague.

- Keep people informed. Keep a public scorecard on your group. Post targets and monthly progress on the bulletin board.

- Ask coworkers for their opinions and viewpoints. Share problems with them. That will demonstrate respect and trust.

- Involve people in planning. Next time a big project lands on your desk, call in all the people involved and plan together.

- Make heroes of other people. Publicize the work of team members. Shine the spotlight on at least one person each day. Who will you spotlight first?

Encourage the Heart

- Say "thank you." Write "You Made My Day" memos. Set a numerical target. Write ten thank-you notes every week, praising people for jobs well done. If you can't find ten things to praise, look harder.

- Be creative with rewards. Make fun and imagination your bywords. Give a giant light bulb to the person who has the best idea of the month. Or a chocolate kiss to a person who makes the office run "sweetly." Tailor ideas to your unique team.

- Provide feedback about results. Feedback is critical. The sooner the better. It can be a "well done" for meeting a target or a detailed debriefing session with a team about how the latest project went and what team members learned.

- Be personally involved. If you don't attend the staff parties and celebrations, you're sending a message that you're not interested or involved.

- Be in love with what you are doing. Keep the magic alive.

The Journey Continues: Ten Ways to Keep Your Leadership Development Alive

So you're back on the job. The pressure is on, deadlines loom, you have a thousand things to think about. Now comes the big challenge of your leadership journey—translating your new insights and skills into daily practice.

The first days and weeks after the workshop are critical. If you don't begin practicing what you learned right away, the momentum soon fades. The only way to begin is to begin—one small action step at a time.

In the workshop, you committed to a number of specific actions you would take in the following weeks. We hope and trust you have followed through on those commitments and have found reward and inspiration in doing so.

So now what?

On the following pages, we have assembled ten simple ideas for taking the next steps in your journey. There is at least one action idea for each of The Five Practices®. We invite you to read them over, choose one that appeals, and do it! Then choose another, or come up with ideas of your own.

Bon voyage!

Ten Ways to Keep Leadership Alive

1. Plan your next Personal Best.

   Identify a challenging project you want to take on. Plan how you will make this a new Personal Best. How will you create and share your vision, involve and encourage others, Model the Way? You may want to refer back to your Personal-Best worksheet for guidance.

2. Get LPI-Observer feedback.

   In the workshop you rated yourself on The Five Practices®. How would others rate you? Ask your manager about how to get LPI feedback from seven to ten co-workers.

3. Share your team's vision.

   Practice relating your team's vision to your peers by talking about it over lunch, displaying your vision poster in the workplace, adding a vision catch phrase to your slide decks, or inspiring customers by talking to them about what your team is trying to do.

4. Practice teamwork at a project meeting.

   Before you go into your next project or staff meeting, plan how you will build teamwork by:

   - Listening attentively.

   - Asking clarifying questions.

   - Asking how you can contribute.

   - Sharing credit.

   - Letting go of "being right," seeking win-win solutions.

   After the meeting, rate yourself. How did you do? Where could you improve?

5. Have lunch with a "stranger."

   Stretch yourself by sharing your lunch hour with someone you wouldn't normally socialize with, someone you interface with often but don't know well. Find out about his or her job or team, what's important to him or her personally. You'll be amazed at the payoffs of showing your interest.

6. Emphasize "We."

   It's not only a token of commitment to teamwork and sharing, but it will be noticed and valued.

7. Recognize someone today.

   At the next team meeting, recognize a colleague for a small (or big!) win. Make your reward unique and sincere.

8. Take on a team challenge.

   Get together with your team and review the potential improvement challenges each of you came up with in the workshop. As a team, select one to take on as a team challenge. Consider the following criteria in making your selection:

   - Is it doable by the team without outside help?

   - If outside help is needed, how difficult will it be to obtain?

   - Will it save time or money?

   - Is it worth doing?

   - Does the team feel real enthusiasm for making this change?

9. Live the values out loud.

   Look again at the company's values. How have you lived one of the values in a visible, memorable way? Or what action might you take to express your commitment to one or more of the values?

10. Recommit.

    This workbook should be filled with action ideas you jotted down during the workshop. Review your notes and select three or more ideas you'd like to implement in the next few weeks. Write your commitments in the chart on page 90 of your workbook and make notes about who else needs to be involved.

Share your commitments with a colleague here in the workshop. (This makes it more real; plus, he or she may have some ideas to contribute.)

Then do it.

ABOUT THE AUTHORS

Jim Kouzes and Barry Posner have been working together for more than thirty years, studying leaders, researching leadership, conducting leadership development seminars, and serving as leaders themselves in various capacities. They are coauthors of the award-winning, best-selling book *The Leadership Challenge*, now in its sixth edition. Since its first edition in 1987, *The Leadership Challenge* has sold more than two million copies worldwide, and it is available in twenty-one languages. It has won numerous awards, including the Critics' Choice Award from the nation's book review editors and the James A. Hamilton Hospital Administrators' Book of the Year Award; has been named a Best Business Book of the Year (2012) by *Fast Company*; and was selected as one of the top ten books on leadership in Jack Covert and Todd Sattersten's *The 100 Best Business Books of All Time*.

Jim and Barry have co-authored more than a dozen other award-winning leadership books, including *The Truth About Leadership: The No-Fads, Heart-of-the-Matter Facts You Need to Know*; *Credibility: How Leaders Gain and Lose It, Why People Demand It*; *Encouraging the Heart: A Leader's Guide to Rewarding and Recognizing Others*; *A Leader's Legacy*; *The Student Leadership Challenge*; *Extraordinary Leadership in Australia and New Zealand: The Five Practices That Create Great Workplaces* (with Michael Bunting); *Turning Adversity into Opportunity*; *Finding the Courage to Lead*; *Great Leadership Creates Great Workplaces*; *Making Extraordinary Things Happen in Asia: Applying The Five Practices of Exemplary Leadership* (with Steve DeKrey); and *The Academic Administrator's Guide to Exemplary Leadership*.

They also developed the highly acclaimed *Leadership Practices Inventory* (LPI), a 360-degree questionnaire for assessing leadership behavior, which is one of the most widely used leadership assessment instruments in the world. More than seven hundred research studies, doctoral dissertations, and academic papers have used The Five Practices of Exemplary Leadership framework they developed.

Jim and Barry have received the Association for Talent Development's highest award for their Distinguished Contribution to Workplace Learning and Performance. In addition, they have been named Management/Leadership Educators of the Year by the International Management Council, ranked by *Leadership Excellence* magazine in the top twenty on its list of the Top 100 Thought Leaders, named among the Fifty Top Coaches in the

United States (according to *Coaching for Leadership*), ranked as Top 100 Thought Leaders in Trustworthy Business Behavior by Trust Across America, listed among *HR* magazine's Most Influential International Thinkers, and included among the list of today's Top 50 Leadership Thinkers by *Inc.* magazine.

Jim and Barry are frequent keynote speakers, and each has conducted numerous leadership development programs for corporate and for-purpose organizations around the globe. These include Alberta Health Services, ANZ Bank, Apple, Applied Materials, Association of California Nurse Leaders, AT&T, Australia Institute of Management, Australia Post, Bain Capital, Bank of America, Bose, Camp Fire USA, Charles Schwab, Chevron, Cisco Systems, Clorox, Conference Board of Canada, Consumers Energy, Deloitte & Touche, Dow Chemical, EMQ Families First, Egon Zehnder, Electronic Arts, FedEx, Genentech, Google, Gymboree, Hewlett-Packard, IBM, IKEA, jobsDB Singapore, Johnson & Johnson, Kaiser Foundation Health Plans and Hospitals, Korean Management Association, Intel, Itaú Unibanco, L.L. Bean, Lawrence Livermore National Laboratory, Lockheed Martin, Lucile Packard Children's Hospital, Merck, Monsanto, Motorola, National Head Start Association, Nationwide Insurance, NetApp, Northrop Grumman, Novartis, Nvidia, Oracle, Petronas, Pixar, Roche Bioscience, Siemens, Silicon Valley Bank, Telstra, 3M, Texas Medical Center, TIAA-CREF, Toyota, United Way, Universal Orlando, USAA, Verizon, Visa, Vodafone, Walt Disney Company, Western Mining Corporation, and Westpac. They have lectured at more than sixty college and university campuses.

Jim Kouzes

Is the Dean's Executive Fellow of Leadership, Leavey School of Business at Santa Clara University, and lectures on leadership around the world to corporations, governments, and nonprofits. He is a highly regarded leadership scholar and an experienced executive; *The Wall Street Journal* cited him as one of the twelve best executive educators in the United States. In 2010, Jim received the Thought Leadership Award from the Instructional Systems Association, the most prestigious award given by the trade association of training and development industry providers. He was listed as one of *HR* magazine's Most Influential

International Thinkers for 2010 through 2012, named one of the 2010 through 2016 Top 100 Thought Leaders in Trustworthy Business Behavior by Trust Across America and honored as one of its Lifetime Achievement recipients in 2015, cited by the Association of Corporate Executive Coaches as the 2015 International Executive Coach Thought Leader of Distinction, and selected by Global Gurus as one of the Top 30 Leadership Gurus in 2015. In 2006, Jim was presented with the Golden Gavel, the highest honor awarded by Toastmasters International. Jim served as president, CEO, and chairman of the Tom Peters Company from 1988 through 2000 and prior to that, he led the Executive Development Center at Santa Clara University (1981–1988). Jim founded the Joint Center for Human Services Development at San Jose State University (1972–1980) and was on the staff of the School of Social Work, University of Texas. His career in training and development began in 1969 when he conducted seminars for Community Action Agency staff and volunteers in the war on poverty. Following graduation from Michigan State University (BA degree with honors in political science), he served as a Peace Corps volunteer (1967–1969). Jim can be reached at jim@kouzes .com.

Barry Posner, Ph.D.

Is the Accolti Endowed Professor of Leadership at the Leavey School of Business, Santa Clara University, where he served as dean of the school for twelve years. He has been a distinguished visiting professor at Hong Kong University of Science and Technology, Sabanci University (Istanbul), and the University of Western Australia. At Santa Clara he has received the President's Distinguished Faculty Award, the school's Extraordinary Faculty Award, and several other teaching and academic honors. Barry has been named one of his nation's top management/leadership educators by the International Management Council, recognized as one of the Top 50 leadership coaches in America and Top 100 Thought Leaders in Trustworthy Business Behavior, ranked among the Most Influential HR Thinkers in the world, and listed among the Top Leadership and Management Experts in the world by *Inc.* magazine. An internationally renowned scholar and educator, Barry has authored or co-authored more than one hundred research and practitioner-focused articles. He currently serves on the editorial advisory board for the *Leadership & Organization Development Journal* and the *International Journal of Servant-Leadership* and received the Outstanding Scholar Award for Career Achievement from the *Journal of Management Inquiry.*

Barry received his BA with honors in political science from the University of California, Santa Barbara; his MA in public administration from The Ohio State University; and his PhD in organizational behavior and administrative theory from the University of Massachusetts Amherst. Having consulted with a wide variety of public and private sector organizations worldwide, Barry also works at a strategic level with a number of community-based and professional organizations. He has served on the board of directors of EMQ FamiliesFirst, the Global Women's Leadership Network, the American Institute of Architects (AIA), Big Brothers/ Big Sisters of Santa Clara County, the Center for Excellence in Nonprofits, Junior Achievement of Silicon Valley and Monterey Bay, Public Allies, San Jose Repertory Theater, Sigma Phi Epsilon Fraternity, as well as publicly traded and start-up companies. Barry can be reached at bposner@scu.edu.